A Walk by the Sea

(A Collection of Life)

Poems by

Thomas Hagan

Parson's Porch Books

www.parsonsporchbooks.com

A Walk by the Sea

ISBN: Softcover 978-1-951472-53-5

Copyright © 2020 by Thomas Hagan

All rights reserved. No part of this book may be reproduced or transmitted in any form or by any means, electronic or mechanical, including photocopying, recording, or by any information storage and retrieval system, without permission in writing from the publisher.

*In loving memory
of my wife
Susan Thielen Hagan*

Acknowledgements

I would like to begin by thanking my daughter, Laura Hagan Sullivan, for providing the photo that was used for the cover of this book. She has provided endless hours of support during the completion of this book. Her assistance is greatly appreciated. I am also indebted to my friend, Bill Braitsch who provided technical support in the completion of this book. His assistance cannot be measured in words alone. Lastly, I would like to thank my fellow writer, Dr. Paul Saluk. He provided constant encouragement and inspired me to be a better writer in the process. I will forever be grateful to him for his friendship.

Contents

A Walk by the Sea	11
A Beginning	12
A Better Day	13
A Choice of Priority	14
A Dance without End	15
A Dove Is Gone!!	16
Adventure	17
A Hiding Place	18
A Label	19
Always There	20
A Magic Carpet	21
A Meaning without Meaning	22
A Memory or a Fruit?	23
A Mighty Good Train	24
A Moment	25
A More Permanent Sand	26
A New Song	27
An Ode to Winter	28
Another Beautiful Day	29
Another Day	30
Another Good Day	31
Any Day is a Better Day	32
Any Tears?	33
A Pawn in Life	34
A Poem of Courage	35
A Renewed Spirit	36
A River	37
Arlie Macadoolie	38
Artwork in the Garden	39
A Satchel of Sunshine	40
Autumn	41
Autumn Lost	42
A Vision	43
A Wonderful Treat	44
Beauty	45
Beauty before My Eyes	46
Beauty on Display	47
Because You Are You	48
Be Happy	49
Better Fish to Fry	50

Better Times, Before the No More	51
Birds	52
Blessings	53
Bliss	54
Bongo! Bongo! Bongo!	55
Boom! Boom! The Waltz Is Running Out of Time	56
Broken Compass	57
Busy-Busy- Busy	58
Change	59
Changing Times	60
Choose Listening and Knowledge	61
Choose One Day at a Time	62
There is never just a finish line but just one day at a time	62
Chop Chop	63
Closeness	64
Cold Winter Is Knocking on the Door	65
Colors	66
Colors and Petals	67
Confusion or Maybe A Tattoo	68
Cooler Times	69
Cross Country Skiing	70
Cultures	71
Custom Made	72
Dancing	73
Delightful Nature	74
Dreams	75
Dreams Can Take You to A Better Place	76
Dreams of the Past and the Way Things Used to Be	77
Drifting	78
Driftwood	79
Drums and Messages in My Ear	80
Dusty Miller	81
Eat Well My Friend	82
Enamored or Ode to A Beautiful Lady	83
Escape	84
Everything Is Just Fine	85
Face in the Mirror	86
Fading Fast	87
Fall	88
Fallen Branches	89
Fast-Moving Train	90

Flexibility of the Mind	91
Flowers in My Garden	92
Freedom	93
Freedom Speaks	94
Friend or Foe	95
Garden of Caring and Love	96
Garden of Roses	97
Get Hold of Your Self	98
Glow a/k/a happy	99
Gone Again	100
Good Fortune	101
Goose Bumps	102
Gray	103
Green	104
Happiness	105
Happiness Is the Goal	106
Here	107
Holding on For Better Days	108
Hollywood	109
Hope	110
Hope for Better Days	111
Maybe better days are in the wind and we can all win	111
I Always Knew Them	112
I Had a Beautiful Dream	113
Nostalgia	114
Tears	115
The Canoe and the River	116
The Ground Is Not So Bad	117
There are so many lobbyists to greed, and parties to attend	117
The Last Dance	118
The Mountain Road	119
The No Mores!	120
The Waves and the Sand	121
What does it take to fill an Empty Heart?	122
About the Author	123

A Walk by the Sea

A walk on the sands along the sounding waves of the sea
There is always time for the serenity in this walk for you and me
A gentle breeze is always a present as the walk proceeds
It's a two-mile journey to visit the little town of small white houses along the sea
The sea birds are all lifting into the air or landing on the sand in our walk by the sea
The air produces a pureness and is easy to breathe
You can walk as bristly as you please, or slow down and enjoy what you see
It's a wonderful place to be in this walk by the sea
The quietness has a way of calming the soul and taking the cares away
There is an avalanche of peace, and everything become beautiful in your mind
Time passes all too quickly as there is so much to see
High tide is still hours away so there is time to appreciate all the beauty we see
A place to return to, time and time again, as if it was for the first time

A Beginning

Love is always a mystery that plays out well, sometimes on the screen
Is screen love really love, or only make believe, or a fantasy of the mind
Does anyone know with certainty all the parameters of the beauty of love
What words snuggle well under the umbrella of love, and paints a picture of understanding?
Does love make you happy, or can I say, please don't be obsessed with a false reality?
Must a reminder play on your mind that only you can make you happy
Yes, love is a relationship, but isn't life's foundations build around this complicated word?
Are we not here as an abiding hand in hand to dance in partnership with relationships?
Relationships can develop into sprinkles of love, but relationships are just a beginning of beginnings
Relationships and maybe the magic of love can grow, but maybe it is always a work in progress
Love is only the platform to be weaved into something special and magnificent, but always a beginning of beginnings

A Better Day

Every time I get a little depressed with the things as they are
It seems there are so many nice people moving my way
There are smiles and laughter always near by
And people opening doors and holding it awhile
There colors are a blend of white, black, yellow, and red
The accents never seem to be the same
There are people who seem to remain a stray
There doesn't seem to be that many as the nice people come into play
Return the smiles and join the laughter, and allow this to be a better day

A Choice of Priority

Choose your battles one by one
Don't become confused
Choose the battles wisely
Let the battles gently unfold
Few are worth the fight
Over reaction is always in sight
It's the important battles my friend
That we must keep in sight
Ignore most battles
Priorities are the struggle
It's only the few battles that win the fight

A Dance without End

There a time to dance, and the time is always
Reaching out and the feet begin to move
The hands are in the air, and you begin to sing
No partner it matters not because it's only temporary
Soon a partner appears from across the room
Moving in your direction and dancing all the way
Embracing you and the Tango begins
The body movements are if they are only one
The evening begins and there appears to be no end
The tango is more than a dance, but an expression of love
Your mind surfing is in constant motion, and joy fills the soul
Anticipate tomorrow, as the dance will begin again

A Dove Is Gone!!

The dove came to my garden, but just for a short stay
The dove was small and only beginning to feel the freedom of being on its own
The dove appeared one morning, and my concern was maybe only the ground was its refuge
Was it possible that flight was not possible today, or was it the nourishment of my garden that beckoned my little dove?
There was grass to eat and seeds seem to be more than enough to store up strength for another day
The beautiful garden had a shower of leaves to provide coolness, and a shelter from the heat
A stream of water in the little pond was refreshing wetness for its beak a day later, much to my delight, as a storm was approaching; she took flight for the comfort of a tree
My thought was that my dove was gone, but each day she reappeared in my garden in the early morning hours for another day's stay
Yesterday, she flew away in the evening hour, and my sadness was mixed
With happiness; as the dove had gone, but maybe the dove had found the way
Maybe, just maybe, the strength was now there after days in the garden, and now the time for flight was right
I go out every morning to view my garden to view the beauty of the plants and flowers in bloom
The reality is that my little dove may never be in my garden again, but maybe another bird may find their way for a short stay

Adventure

Trees and rivers have always been my friends
A place to walk in the shade of a tree covered lane
A trip down a river to refresh your memories and dreams
They often fill each breathe with an abundance of fresh air
There is always a stump to rest on in the tree covered lane
There are sand bars on the side of the river to place your boat
Take your time among the trees, the river or a stream
Enjoy nature for all its beauty that it provides
A renewed spirit will soon arise, and lift you up and hold you there
A trail or river with all its twist and turns will hold you in its arms
Don't guess or try to remember the way it goes
Be surprised as if you have never been there before
Make it an adventure and enjoy the day no matter where it leads you

A Hiding Place

The walls were shaking and the floors were shifting
As I walked around the mall
The sights around me were something to behold
Many large figures were moving in all direction
Fright was consuming my soul
My body moved from one hiding place to another
It is a search for survival, as I run from the mall

A Label

When is a friend a friend, and not a person just passing by?
Acquaintance, are so many, and so uncountable at the moment
Will any of the acquaintances every enter into the realm of the title of friend?
People often tell me that friends are rare, and can be counted on one hand
How much does a person have to like someone for them to be counted as a friend?
Is it a matter of looks, intelligence, kindness, favors, gifts, or the listening that creates a friend?
What barometer should one use to measure when a person can become your friend?
Are the calendar pages needed to set a magic time when the glories of friendship become thine?
As I become older, and am asked to name my friends, then hesitation appears to set in
Upon reflection, it become to mind that it is no different than
when I was young
Yes, the definition and requirement of naming a friend, can often be a daunting task
It has entered my mind that the word, friend, is just another label, and has no place in a relationship

Always There

Living stones are always there
How do we get them to move without any fear?
No involvement or retreat in their caves as a hide away
Agree or not to agree is no matter to the living stones
They live in the confinement of their own solitary souls
The reactionaries are always there
They place their misconceptions, and fears on the table
The sky is always falling, and the bogeyman is very real
They beg for change at every turn, but they are unsure as to where to go
They are a bundle of confusion at every turn
Their happiness is a distortion of reality and the truth

A Magic Carpet

A magic carpet ride to the magic city by the sea
Yes, I am going to Miami for a few days.
I can't seem to stay away too long.
It is time to jump up and down and wander all around.
It is time to see the sights of old, and remissness about where my life was in times of old.
The old neighborhoods, schools, and places of play are a must for me to see

A Meaning without Meaning

People do not seem to know where they are at
Searching for things that do not exist
Days pass by without meaning
Clouds overhead confusing the minds
The end is always near, but never there
Is there a reason for people to share?
The fog is there, but is there anyone there?
If there, is then do they really care?
Where is the march that is worth the while?
The march seems to be in circles, and a waste of time
People seem to be becoming dizzy, and they are all falling down

A Memory or a Fruit?

I remember the Rose Apple from the days that have long past
It smelled of Rose Water when I placed it in my mouth
The Rose Apple tree was only encountered once by me
The fruit appeared inviting as I plucked it from the tree
That was so well hidden in my memory, and yet it appeared to me today
I look forward to again plucking a Rose Apple from that wonderful tree
Maybe someday you may have the opportunity to enjoy this delight
Don't pass the Rose Apple Tree by without taking at least one from the tree
The joy that was once mine could be shared by you
There is little doubt that you will enjoy this little Rose Apple as much as me

A Mighty Good Train

Are we up or are we down?
Maybe we are just turned around
Turn around, turn around, and spin around once more
Its one step forward and three steps back
Close the doors or open them wide
Maybe we need to know who is knocking on the door its
war here and war there, and no peace in sight
Why are the workers siting on the bench?
Jobs, jobs, jobs, but there are no jobs
Money running short and cupboard is running low
Alcohol, joints, powder, and pills are filling the void
Despair and gloom are coating the land as many are falling all around
Hope, they say, will bring you through, but what does that mean to the person on the ground?
Change is coming, but all it's brought in the past is more greed, and lies to cover their tracks
Looking for the future and don't turn back, but the future looks like the back
Maybe good change is coming; so be prepared to ride a better train down the tracks
Get aboard! Get aboard! I see a shining light, and this train is a mighty good train

A Moment

A moment is a special thing
Appreciate and savor the joys it can bring
Wrap it in the cloth of happiness and sail on
The moment is so fleeting, but it can return
The times may be dire, and the moment of happiness returns
A saving grace by the moment of time
Hold it for only a second, and the freshness reappears
Life is all about relationships, and the capture of the moments of time

A More Permanent Sand

Coulda-Woulda-Shoulda, but the game of change was really never begun
The marches occurred with great frequency, and the bang bang never stopped
Nothing ever changed because the before, and after were always the same
The winners were always the winners and the loser were always the same
The word and idea of change were just things written in the sand
The sand was washed away to the sea of time, and soon forgotten
for a time
New the marches began again, and the rallies were always loud with words to be heard
The changes were only the same old platitudes that had been played, and heard before
The new marches and rallies were interspersed with renewed enthusiasm
This time things would be different and results would come to pass It was always mostly the younger crowds that were not familiar with the loses of the before
Renewed vigor brought excitement, and the belief that this time things would be different
The ideas and changes were soon bought out and destroyed by the same old powers as always before
It's always been pay for play, and those without the resources never get to play
The sandboxes of change became smaller and smaller and soon went away
Quietness and disillusion soon set in, and the crowds and sounds, were as they were never there at all
There was peace in the valley, but only temporarily, and next time maybe the sounds of change would really occur
Sometimes hope is the only reward and changes will only have to wait for their time in a more permanent sand

A New Song

A new song is in the air, and what a beautiful song it is
The birds are chirping away in such delightful harmony
It is the wakeup call of spring, and the silence of winter is behind us
The weather is bringing the earth a warmness as winter has passed
The leaves are dressing the trees with a fresh greenness
The gardens are beginning to sprout flowers, vegetables, and an array of sights
It is time to take that long awaited walk along the pathways of spring
There is a welcoming sign everywhere that the roads ahead are new and good
Rejoice and enjoy the sounds, beauty, and awakening of spring

An Ode to Winter

The leafs are falling on the ground
Fall is almost over and winter will soon begin
The frost is in the air and sweater time is near
A burst of energy here and there
It's cross country skiing time
That has always been dear to me
A trip to the back county where few have tread
Thoughts of snow trails and high altitudes once a gain
My eagerness is getting the best of me
Back country skiing is more than just great exercise to me
It brings out a relaxation of its own
The eyes move from direction to direction
All the sights are beautiful in their own way
Stop wherever you like because there is no need to hurry
Each season has a beauty of its own
Accept each season as a blessing for you to own

Another Beautiful Day

The sun is out, but not too hot
The birds are chirping and singing beautiful songs
My garden is in full bloom, and what a beautiful sight
It is time to take a long walk along the tree covered trail
The air is fresh and still a little crisp
People greet me with a soft hello
Their faces seem to always have a smile
The quietness brings on a tranquility of its own
It is now time to start for home
There are always things to do
It is always about priorities my friends
Many things never have to be done
Keep the beautiful days going by calling a good friend?
Take as much rest as you can, because tomorrow will bring you another beautiful day
It is though there is no other world out there

Another Day

It seems to be a merry-go-round with no end in sight
Everyone saying it's not their fault
Open your eyes because it's everyone's fault
People killing and robbing in so many ways
Few seem to care and only for awhile
The merry-go-round seems to be going faster
People screaming to let them off
But no one seems to want it to stop
Collateral damage, isn't that the way
People say if it's isn't me then let it be
Apathy and aggression are all mixed together
Let us talk about it another day

Another Good Day

Enjoy each day because each day is all you may ever have
Meaningless little words may have no meaning at all
Worrying about the future is not a plan, but just worrying
Take care of today, and live well my friend
Today has enough variables and the future has not yet been unfurled
Surround yourself with cheerful people and let the nay Sayers go their own way
Seek the fresh air of life and thinking good thoughts is well worth the while
Remember the only time you failed is the last time you tried
Remember also lifting people up is a blessing you will never forget
Let others be the storm clouds, but for you it's just another blessing being you

Any Day is a Better Day

Tomorrow is going to be a better day
You just wait and see
A setting of rights from wrongs
A glow in the spirit as people begin to smile your way
Warming and heart felt ideas will take their rightful place
A step in the right direction as the old is pushed away
Tomorrow can be everything that we want it to be
Wake up with an attitude of a good and cheerful face
Tomorrow is waiting for you to open the book with thoughts of good
The hands of good are willing to hold your hand and lead you on to a better place
Don't turn back, but only move ahead, and greet tomorrow with its plans of good
Tomorrow is just a day away, so be prepared to embrace it as it presents a better day

Any Tears?

There are enough tears in the world
So cry not!
But weather the storm
Thing the wonderful thoughts of yesteryears
Think the thought of shining days that are ahead
There will always be bumps in the road of life
Don't abide with the bumps but ride them like magic carpets
A magic carpet to the better days that lie ahead
Look ahead to the good thoughts that will set you free
Free from the gloom, but place yourself on a hill that sees only the good

A Pawn in Life

Are we only a pawn in life?
We need clean air but greed says stay out of the way
Pollution is good for the economy
It's all about money, don't you know anything
Smokestacks are continuing to rise and CO_2 is moving toward the sky
We need clean water, but greed says it's not your problem anyway
Pollution is good for the economy
Minimum wage isn't so bad
Food stamps are waiting for you so don't be sad
Health care, you don't need that
That is something for people that can afford
You say crime and drugs are ruining your neighborhood
You say you can't move out, and people of greed say that sounds sad
The rich get richer and the poor get poorer
Isn't that the way it has always been
Get to work and clean those pans
Because minimum wage is almost in your hands
You say you want a better way of life
Did you forget you are only a pawn in the game?

A Poem of Courage

Ode to the Immigrant
I am the immigrant that has traveled for miles and miles
My goal always lies ahead, and freedom for a life reborn
The life I was born into was just a temporary stay
It was a stopping place until my strength was renewed
The road ahead is winding through many twists and turns
No wall, river, or forces ahead will prevent me from my goal
My will is strong because to stay behind was not my way
A better life is just ahead for me; so I will keep going on my way
There is a better land ahead, and I cannot tarry long
The people in the new land will accept me as their own
This is what I have been told, and encourages me to travel on
That is what I believe, and that is what keeps me strong
Freedom and a chance to work is all I ask for in this new land
Is there any reason to hold back, when the promise of so much lies ahead?
My feet are moving again, and I will not stop until I reach my new land

A Renewed Spirit

Winter is on the way, and the leaves will soon begin to fall
The leaves will be beautiful with their reds, browns, and golds
There will be a picture everywhere for one, and all to see
The chill will soon begin to fill the air and its sweater time again
Fall always allows newness, as the summer heat fades away
There is easiness about the fall, which allows us to prepare for what's ahead
It's a time to relax and reflect on what was, and what may come our way
It's a time to spend more time outside before winter comes into play
My feet shuffle among the fallen leaves, as they make their own patterns on the ground
It's time to take the time to enjoy the beauty that's all around
Fall, I welcome thee every year, as you bring me a renewed spirit, and more hope for tomorrow

A River

I have a thirst deep within me for a return to the river
A river that was a apart of me and so many memories from long ago
Those cherished memories that present nothing but a love for the water and natures abound
There is no loneliness with all the beauty that nature can afford
The canoe moves thru the waters as if a part of the river itself
A part that has always been and always will be
The river, nature, and the canoe are one
The trees, flowers, and animal life are all present for the view
Each bend in the river creates a new awakening, as the water continues to flow
Paddle or paddle not, because the current is always ready to move you along
Each day in a river's life is a new adventure, and always worth the while

Arlie Macadoolie

Arlie Macadoolie where have you been?
It's been so long; since I don't know when
You use to be a friend of mine, a friend of old
And our times were spent well together
I thought of you often and I hope you are well
Your travels must have been many
I pray that safety was there to clothe you from all harm
Some day we will meet again, and remember the old times
yes, remember the old times as if they were today
Are you still dancing and prancing along life's way?
You were a dapper little fellow; as I remember well
Always smiling and cheerful
And making other people's day a better place to be
Yes, Arlie Macadoolie, I remember you well

Artwork in the Garden

Butterflies are nature's artwork in an array of masterful colors
Their flight is an aeronautical curiosity with every move
They always add to a garden's beauty
As if they were beautiful flags fluttering in the wind
And keeps the eyes in a frequent gaze as they move about
The colors defy the imagination of even the most creative
The gardens appreciate these visitors of so many colors
And greet them as if they were an old friend
They always leave an impression that will return again
The next visit may bring coats of colors from new butterfly friends
The surprise each day is always worth the wait
The garden seems to stretch out and offer them a place to land
Continue your flight my butterfly friends
But you can stay as long as you like

A Satchel of Sunshine

A satchel of sunshine is a gift that keeps on giving.
The sunshine is all wrapped up in you waiting to be released.
A satchel filled with sunshine of love and caring each for one another A happy outreach of a beautiful smile, a handshake, or a hug may be appearing
Always carry that satchel close by for the time is always near for its release of good things inside
A welcome hello is not that difficult to do
Remember it's the little things that create the joys that place the happiness in our lives
Reach out because it is right thing to do, and you will receive the love and caring in return
Respect for others allows that same respect to come to you.
Do the right thing and open that satchel but remember to open it wide

Autumn

The joy of autumn
And the freshness of the air
The beauty of the leaves
As they fall at my feet
The multicolored carpet
Spreads itself around
My voice can be heard
Praising God for the picture
That is painted on the ground

Autumn Lost

My favorite season is no more
Where is my beautiful autumn weather?
Summer has now passed me by, and moved into winter
The colors came in a day, and the leaves fell so quickly to the ground
No global warming the fools say
It has always been that way as they scream at me
It is so painful to see autumn taken away from me
No time for sweaters, as my winter coat now covers me
How could people be so foolish?
But then, they have always been that way

A Vision

I bought a ticket just the other day
The man at the counter said, son, where do you want to go
I told him with gleefulness in my voice, America, sir
Son that is mighty expensive ticket to buy
I was concerned and uneasy; as I asked, sir, why is that?
There is so little left of it, and rest is hard to find
You may be riding that train for an awful long time
I thought about that for a long, long time
Finally I reached out, and placed the money in his hands
That train traveled for miles, and miles with no America in sight
There were traces here and there, but no America, in sight
I asked the conductor, where did America go?
It unraveled overtime because greed came like a hurricane into play
The caring and thinking became a thing of the past
Everyone became a stranger, even unto themselves
The skies became a cast of dark grays, and things began to die
The conductor told me to not give up on the ride
Stay aboard because I had paid my fare for a long, long ride
The days went on and on, but I never got tired
My vision was, that soon, America would come into view

A Wonderful Treat

Spinach, turnip greens, and broccoli are a real treat
Mama, where are the squash and mustard greens?
Can somebody pass the bean sprouts?
Carrots are crunchy little things, and what a delight
Even a tree picked apple can create a flavorful explosion in my mouth
Push away the meats because it's not for me
Bring on some more vegetables and fill my plate
The green, yellow, red, orange, and brown
The colors of fruits and vegetables are too many to count
They are just the beginning of what makes us go around
The day starts off right and ends with abound
If you eat those fruits and vegetables that are all around

Beauty

How does beauty express itself?
But what is beauty before we begin?
Can it be seen, felt, heard, imagined, or is it only an allusion?
Is beauty so real that it moves the heart in mysterious ways?
Is beauty an idea, a picture, an emotion, a dream, or an elusive undefinable?
Is it important that we understand or define beauty?
Why don't we just embrace it as what it is, beauty?

Beauty before My Eyes

Beauty before my eyes
Where the sun shines and
Waters flow and palm trees grow
The land where everything seems bright
The future is always today
Never a dark cloud in the sky
The horizons are always reachable
Learning is enjoyable even as the sun beckons one to push the books aside
    The place of all so many cultures
There to blend and make friends
The return is always in my heart
And the beauty is always in my mind

Beauty on Display

Many things can only be described through the eyes
The eyes paint a picture in your mind which can last forever
A garden of azaleas stretching over the landscape
Covering the ground with their beauty is a new picture everyday
Flowers unfold and present themselves in a manner as yet unseen before
Calmness comes over the soul as never before
And develops a new awakening in the appreciation of beauty
The serenity is abounding as the walk begins through the garden
Each season has a new showcase to welcome the eyes as never before
The spring air is refreshing as the flowers are all aglow
The fragrance of new growth is everywhere
The flowers seem to offer a curtsy as one walks by
Only touch the flower with your eyes
There are many others on their way to see the display

Because You Are You

A beautiful day is every day when you remain you
Troubles and sorrow will come, but you will remain beautiful because
you are you
Sunshine will appear in your life, and it will always be brighter where you are;
because you are you
Happiness is in you, because you are you
Others will smile and their faces will glow because you are near,
and because you are you

Be Happy

Glow
Stretch out the arms and offer a hug today
There are people waiting for your expression of caring
Smiles are always a welcome sight
Walk with love in your heart and people will feel it
Say something nice because it's the right thing to do
Yes, you are suffering and so are we all
There is always others suffering more just around the corner
Giving is a lifetime project and not just for today
Lift people up and never push them down
The sun is always shining when you are all aglow

Better Fish to Fry

Better fish to fry or chalk it up
Should I care or say I don't?
The monuments are falling down everywhere
but, the names on the forts are still there
Should the names remain or go away?
What is your say today?
Do you have fish to fry or do you want to chalk it up?
You say you don't know what I'm writing about
That is not my challenge so figure it out

Better Times, Before the No More

There was a time when times were better
That was before people were gathered together
Evil born and often remained throughout the time of life
Wars and destruction were the themes they enjoyed most
Treat their neighbors to the blade of the sword
If that was not enough then bring in the guns and cannons to finish the rest
Love and compassion are stories in books
Bring on the greed that satisfies the thirst for more greed
Destroy the enemies until there are no more
The earth is now barren with a redness covering the ground
Now it's time to drink the water, but there is no more
The ground is baked solid, and the sun continues to bake more
It's the greed for more, but now there is no more

Birds

Did you ever look skyward recently at the birds in flight?
Their wings spread wide as they glide through the air
My imagination sometimes allows me to fly just as high
My arms are spread wide as I wonder what it's like to be a bird in flight
Free from the ground, and the landing can be at your choosing
Food appears to be everywhere, as it's so easy to spot so high in the air
There should be no need for hunger, and now it's time for a refreshing drink
Birds appear as a picture painting as they dart here and there
Freedom is wherever they want it to be
Fly my birds and fill the air, as my eyes will never tire of thy beauty

Blessings

Blessings flow in their own time and way
Sometimes they don't appear to be blessings at all
Doors shut so tightly and lock you out
Only with time you realize the lock was a blessing in disguise
Beautiful things will always be coming your way
Sometimes it's difficult to appreciate them until they are on their way out
Look for the good in life because it will be there
Surround yourself with joyfulness and friends of good cheer
There will always be nay Sayers, but don't let them engage you
with their doubts
The light and horizon is always on the other side of the hill

Bliss

Why are they there at the top of the political heap?
Maybe they are intelligent, but maybe they are not
Intelligent or not is no matter; because ignorance is the force in play
The dendrites and neurons are doing a slow dance, or maybe even a waltz
Their ignorance is replaced daily by the their puppet masters
Say this or say that; then vote the way the strings are pulled
Voters are the pawns in the scheme; because they don't matter
The play has been written before the games begin
Tell them what the puppet masters wants them to say
Lying is only an artful manner of speech
Confuse them with dribble, and say the things they want to hear
Collect your paycheck and enjoy your life
Remember the puppet masters have you in their embrace
Remember it's just another day, and ignorance in this game can be bliss

Bongo! Bongo! Bongo!

Bongo! Bongo! Bongo!
Bongo! Bongo! Bongo! The sound is getting louder
The drums are beating faster and the crescendo is coming into play
Confusion is developing and the nation is wrapping itself in fear
There is nowhere to go and nowhere to hide
The warning was everywhere, but heads in the sand ruled the day
The puzzle people have taken us apart, and have lost the pieces along the way
People are crying out we have lost our way, and the puzzle is in disarray
It's hard to find the way when the drums are beating louder
Bongo! Bongo! Bongo! Settle down we pray, and let us find the pieces
We had so much time before, and now the time is short, but confusion rules the day
The puzzle is in so many pieces, and it's hard to make them fit
Should we try or just give up? Bongo! Bongo! Bongo!

Boom! Boom! The Waltz Is Running Out of Time

The waltz of time is closing in as consternation abides in the land
The waltz has been only hype in the hands of the mighty band
Greatness for the few has played for hundreds of years
Slavery played its waltz for three hundred and fifty years
Does 1607 to 1965 ring up a tune in the waltz of time?
Does one hundred million Native Americans dead feel it was the best of times
Do the hungry, homeless, and those without medical care feel the greatness in their time?
Do those with additions feel that going to prison, instead of receiving care; feel the greatness in the waltz of time
The rigged political system that suppresses voters even in today's time
The money flows in to buy every election, but those on the corner cry out can you spare me a dime
Greatness for the few is quickly playing out as the masses are saying it is now their time
It is a new day and time to play a new waltz of time, and more than a chicken in every pot
A new economic system where everyone has a living wage, food on the table, medical care, quality educations, and time for a waltz or two
It is a new day coming where everyone will have a chance to relax, play, and feel that they are really free to be great for the first time
The music is beginning to sound out, as the violins are playing the peoples waltz, and a new day is taking to the dance floor
It's the peoples time and not just for the few

Broken Compass

We are the enemy of ourselves, and the most destructive force
on planet earth
The face in the mirror is just the beginning of the totality of our
own destruction
Leadership is an illusion only written about in storybooks
Scotty has me on hold, but my time is soon to behold, and my beaming up
days are in sight
We are a part of giant spinning wheel riding on the humanity of misfortunes
of our own making
We are too often moving in the direction of a broken compass that is
sending us in the wrong direction
We need to get hold of ourselves and ride the wave of reality that will move
us into the wraps of betterment
We hold ourselves in the bondage of our own making, but
tomorrow will surely be a better day
The starting point is with us, and the optimism of change is the correct way
to go
Hold steady my friend, because there is a real rainbow at the end waiting to
be found

Busy-Busy- Busy

Busy-busy-busy is the order of the day
I have got to keep busy, and there is no time to play
Yes, it's time to plan my garden, because spring is on the way
It's flowers only this year, and with a rainbow of colors for display
The flowers and colors are presenting a show of their own in my mind
There are so many to choose from; so my manner is in a busy way
Busy-busy-busy is the only way, when so many things must be done
It's gardening tools, and food for the plants in order to make the flowers grow
It is all worth the while because spring will welcome my flowers with gentle showers
The day will come, and the flowers will unfold before my eyes
The busy-busy-busy was all worth the while as the flowers sprinkled their love on me

Change

Change never is a standalone thing
Change ripples through the landscape with a mind of its own
Change touches everything in its quake
Change can be a good thing, but don't count on it
Change for change's sake can be ignorance at the door
Change brings consequences, and you can't count them on your toes
Change effects changes here and there, and then rolls along
Those changes in turn do their thing, and then only escalate more change
It is difficult to predict the consequences of change until sometimes it's too late
Change cannot be placed in a bottle or enclosed in a cage
Change can move in many directions at once
Change can even change people into something you are not
The tentacles of change dance across the land
The change occurs often much faster than people can understand
Change is coming our way today just as it did yesterday
Embrace change, but always be prepared to place a bridle on it
Change needs controls and directions long before it gets out of hand

Changing Times

Women! Women! Give them a cheer, and be glad they are here
It's no, surprise that a woman is in first place
It's been building for a long time at a rapid pace
It's not about anyone in particular, but woman kind
Not so long ago the men were filling the colleges with a heavy percent
Today the graduation rate is overwhelming women and growing, and that's a fact
Medical and law students are female with over fifty percent
Vet schools are dominated by women and that's a fact
The rolls keep growing and never standing still
What are the men doing, but dropping out
It's changing the culture, and that's a fact
The women bread winners are moving over the land like an avalanche
It was just a matter of time until the king of the mound would be replaced by woman kind

.

Choose Listening and Knowledge

Listening should never be a lost art
It's not about courtesy, but a reward for you
Learning and listening go hand and hand
There will be learning when you're talking begins
Others have ideas and expression so let them begin
Ask questions and allow their information to come in
Others have knowledge and wisdom for you
I love new knowledge, don't you ?

Choose One Day at a Time

Get on down the road, but always remember to take the roads for you
Any old road will not serve you well because some roads were not meant for you
It's not a matter of whether the road is easy or not, but where you need to go
A bumpy less travelled road is a great road if it favors your goal
Just remember to not take the road that meanders and takes you to your starting place
Don't run away from the road because it challenges to be better than you are
Keep up a steady pace and only rest enough to allow the travel to begin again
There is never just a finish line but just one day at a time

Chop Chop

Chop Chop America because the time is getting late
The right and the left are dangling, but without a resolve
No direction, but only a bundle of confusion
The shining city on the hill is still without a home
Knock knock and there is a sound of sleep on the hill
The hour is late, but the deep sleep must go on
The world turns around and around, but America sleeps on
Chop chop is ringing out loud and clear, but to no avail
Chop chop because the time is getting late

Closeness

When you are only two blocks away; it feels like you are miles away.
It's difficult to keep my heart under control
It seems that dreams are always of a time when together and together are more than a dream
A time when the future is not so far away
Parting is more than parting, but a distance of strain
Remembrances come into play, but they will never suffice for the real thing
Closeness brings unity and a place in my heart that is everlasting

Cold Winter Is Knocking on the Door

Winter is coming on faster each day
And the welcome mat is already on doorstep
My blanket covered with beautiful wolves comforts me
The snow will fall soon enough, and it is time for winter clothes
A snow-covered ground brings on a silence of its own
It is time for the warmth by a fireplace, and reflecting on the wonders of the past
Yes, there were so many good times, as I place the bad times so far away
It is time to pull a good book from my shelves, because reading is such a gift for the mind
Sometimes it's a new book that has never been read or an old one waiting for my attention once again
Isolation on a cold winter night is what you make of it, because it is never quite for long
A knock on the door often bring you face to face with a welcome guest
Maybe a warm glass of cider or tea is what is needed
It is all what you make of it, because winter can be a welcome guest all by itself
Enjoy your winter because I may the next one to knock on your door
I don't know if I will bring gifts of good tidings, but only a pleasant story or two
It is time to rejoice because I can tell you there have been many good blessings awaiting you
Good times are ahead so sitting back in that easy chair and read that book by the fire

Colors

Colors that I see all around me are a blessing
The appreciation is worth it all as I see beauty all around me
The colors can match any rainbow, and often even more
The blessing of sight provides a color storm of life every moment of the day
The flowers, trees, streams, rivers, stones, rocks, and all the structures here to see
Place so many of your tribulations aside, and enjoy to the fullness of the sights before you
My eyes arrest upon a painting of many colors that springs forth excitement in my soul
Never take for granted the shows of life before you, as they spring forward in colors
Colors, colors everywhere and more are around the corner waiting for you to see

Colors and Petals

Colors spread their wings as the petals open wide
They spread their beauty before my eyes
The dormant flowers of winter have become alive
The branches express their vigor, and lift the flowers for all to see
The colors are like a beautiful painting with a landscape of their own
The petals dance as the wind gently moves their way
Eyes are fixed and smiles are pronouncing their applause
Spring is here, and the show is here again for all to see
Nature's beauty has no equal; so there is no compare
The glaze brings a refreshing renewal of the soul
The morning walk through the garden is a beautiful way to begin a day
So until tomorrow the memories of the garden moments will enlighten my walk through the day
Whenever I want to retreat from the world, then my concentration reverts to nature, and all of its beauty

Confusion or Maybe A Tattoo

Politics appears to have a right side and left side
Is there no middle, or is it always left, or right?
Is that like driving on the right or left side of the road?
Who created those terms, and what do they really mean?
If the right is right; then are they, always right?
If the left is left; then what are they left of?
Why do we have a middle of the road if no one ever there?
Is it possible for a person to be on the left, and right?
You know, depending on the issue at the time
Are labels permanent or can a person change their mind?
Why are there labels, or can't a person move about from time to time?
Should we tattoo people with a left or right, so that we can better understand?
The tattoo could be a warning sign as to what lies ahead
Can a person wear a middle of the road tattoo, or would that confuse the other two?

Cooler Times

Cooler times are ahead as fall brings its veil over us
Fall is welcomed with open arms as the return of a love one
The dues of a long hot summer are now paid, and it's time to move along
The pleasantness of a stroll through the woods will bring a
renewed pleasure
Why can't fall be here all year long because it is my favorite above all?
All the wonders of plants and animals alike find the reward of fall a
gift of delight
The trees are shedding their clothing of leaves, but spring will all so
soon bring them back
There is no painting more beautiful than the array of colors brought to us
as if the trees is on fire
My arms are open wide for fall, and I embrace it with my heart and soul
each year with spirit of goodness

Cross Country Skiing

Cross country skiing is exciting, and the body is all aglow
Let's view the beautiful sights as we go
The snow is still falling, and provides a crispness in the air
Stop where you may, and enjoy whatever you see
There is no hurry because we have all day
The terrain can be gentle, or more challenging you see
You make the decision as to where to go
The trees are all covered with snow
Some is falling on the path as the winds blows
It's time to rest; so stop whenever you will
Soon it's time to travel again where we have never been
The skiing will be over for today, but the return can never be too soon

Cultures

What is right, what is wrong?
It is the culture you know
I still do not understand where do you live?
Is it by the ocean or by the sea?
Maybe in some distant land No,
I live in the U. S. of A.
Now I am confused
You live in a land that is culture free
Free from this and free from that
A land of many cultures
This confuses even me

Custom Made

Words can be a beautiful shower that can free the soul from so much hurt
Sometimes silence can replace words, and stand alone as tender care package
Sometimes just being there is all that is needed to relieve another's pain
Even the strong are at times weakened by the events wrapped upon them
Everyone has their own needs, and can only be met if tailor made for them
The inner beings of people are hidden in their minds, so approach lightly
Everyone has their own special weaknesses and strengths
So custom made is the best way to go

Dancing

Dancing dandy, dancing through life
It is always a waltz or a faster movement through the drums?
Do your tire before the dance is done?
Stop and rest a while
You deserve the stay
Do you change the partners all too soon?
Or remain until the dance is done?
Does the life of dance strain you to the bone?
Or do you want to dance on and on?

Delightful Nature

Nature's beauty is such a delight
It's all within sight
The moment of the clouds
The moon shines so bright
The leaves changing colors
The freshness of the air in the mountain meadow
The snow is falling with each snowflake created with its own beautiful design
The rivers flowing over stones so smooth
The waters orchestrating a symphony of sounds
The fragrance of the trees makes the walk so rewarding
The parade of beauty never ends, but only begins

Dreams

Dreams are like clouds
They come and then they go
They are magical and take you to places
You may or may not want to go
The spirit of running in a meadow of wildflowers
The smelling of fresh mountain air
Sadness revisited and tears in the eyes
Love lost in the foolishness of youth
Words remembered that should have never been said
Kindness withheld, or not shared
Embraces and kisses which were always hidden
Many regrets, but there were the good times
The walking in a summer rain and the wetness
Drew us together hand in hand
A time to remember
The sweetness of the evening breeze
You in my lap and softness in our hearts
Whispering the beautiful thoughts
Of the ways things were going to be

Dreams Can Take You to A Better Place

A pillow within a pillow or a dream within a dream
Dreams can run on and on without any reason it seems
One dream flows into another, and there is no connection between the two
Dreams can be scary, or just beautiful flows of majestic gardens of colors
When is a vision a dream, or really a vision, with a deep meaning of understanding something new?
My most beautiful dreaming was a running through a field of wildflowers in a mountain meadow
My favorite dreaming is daydreaming that takes me away from the boredom of the day
Even good things can be just good, and never good enough, to void out my pleasure of daydreaming
Day dreaming is more than an escape from reality, but a bridge to impossible bridges that can expand the mind
Yes, expand the mind to better things than are yet unavailable in a world of torment and distrust
The return to reality can be an undeserved punishment that should have never been showered on you
Trust dreams only unto yourself except in the rarity of the blessing that you meet a dreamer much like yourself
Dreams and visions are more than a hiding place from reality, but and escape to a new and better world
Cover yourself with dreams of wonderment, and float on a never-ending carpet to the better world outside of reality
May sweet dreams and new visions of, a better tomorrow and place, take away the any hurts or sorrows that may fill your place

Dreams of the Past and the Way Things Used to Be

The landfill was bulging higher toward the sky
Plastic bottles and bags by the billions, so goes the count
Toxic chemicals in the lakes and streams, no it's real and not a dream
Chemical for the sugar cane fields now flow into the Sea of Grass
The Everglades is dying, and the water purification is a thing of the past
Fish are dying, and a clean ocean is many years in the past
Greed abides everywhere; because it's the nature of man
The skies are darkening, and the air is heavy with pollution hoovering about
The lungs are struggling, and gasping the filthy air as people die
Birds on the ground, as they fall from the sky
Health care is not about helping people, but money in the bank
Oklahoma is more earthquakes bound than the Pacific Coast
It's fracking time in order to disturb the earth, and turbulence now abounds
Ignorance is the new national anthem and aren't we proud?
Dreams of the past, and the way things used to be

Drifting

Drifting away and going nowhere
Hungry people everywhere
Fat cats sailing everywhere
The top is too far up to see down, so
why worry they are in the crown
Are you sick of being sick?
Don't worry no one cares
Jobs are too far away
They are overseas
You can't see them now, they are long gone
The unemployment lines are long
Don't worry, no one cares

Driftwood

What comes to mind as you see driftwood lying on the shoreline?
Do you ponder about its journey as it found its way for you to see?
Was it pushed into the ocean by a violent storm in a land far away?
Was it a resting place for birds which were flying across the sea?
The decomposition as it traveled it's way is nature's art work on display
The holes and curves which were gnarled into the woods are
beauty unsurpassed
Nature's creatures and the motion of the waves all contributed to the beauty
we see
Allow your eyes to follow the holes and lines in the wood today
Appreciate the craftsmanship because it's a one of a kind, and that's the way
it should be
Leave the wood there for others to see and appreciate
There may be the time when there will be a piece that touches your heart
Treasure that piece and realize that the artists were many
The journey may have been long, and it's not like any other treasure, but
special indeed

Drums and Messages in My Ear

Where did my country go or can I find it over there?
Is it hidden under the umbrella of politics or the dungeons of repression?
Why must I anguish over something that should have never been?
Is greed and selfishness the new playground of life?
Money everywhere but not in sight
Few have it all and is that the plight?
Is it the politic or the system that is the fight?
Did it happen overnight that darkness overcame daylight?
Where are the drums and messages in my ears?
Which will foretell that a new day is here?

Dusty Miller

Dusty Miller was welcomed to my garden today
The silvery gray leaves were all spread in a beautiful display
The lacy leaves keep my eyes in a constant gaze
The other plants smiled broadly as Dusty Miller came marching in
Dusty Miller brought an instant enhancement of beauty to the garden landscape
There are so many choices when adding plants to a garden
Every plant presents its own resume of beauty, and meanings as to why they should be there to
Dusty Miller won the prize today, and I am very glad she did
Every day beckons me to arise early, and stroll through my garden of pure delight

Eat Well My Friend

The fields where the fruits and vegetables grow well and strong
The workers of the field grow weaker as the days go on
Let us visit the meat processing houses along the way
So many undocumented workers are slaving for you and me
This is just a mention of the few places with workers with only the
rights of a slave
The conditions are too often dreadful, and the children working there today
Are there no schools for the children, and only the fields to be tended today?
The wages are small, but the profits from the fields seem to roll along
The good earth they say, but to whom is it good?
The fruits and vegetables flood the shelves and restaurants as well
Can you taste the blood, sweat, and tears as you approach the food?
We eat so well, but do we give a thought as to how the food filled
our plate?
You say greed is good because it's better them than me that work the fields
Enjoy your meals and never consider how the food arrived on your plate

Enamored or Ode to A Beautiful Lady

Enamored, such a beautiful word
Sprinkles of love flowing at every portal
The passion and charm covers like a blanket
Conceal it not, but let it be known
No shame in being enamored
The heart is beating faster
And the speech may be stammered
It's all worth the glory of being enamored

Escape

Escape, but back to what, where, and when?
Can you ever go back except in your dreams and memories of the past?
Movies, video games, music, drinking, drugging, and always count on the weed
Yes, they blanket you with the escape in answer to your plea.
But then then the ugly reality pitched in and brings you back to the challenges of the now
When will the hatred subside, and peace provide a bed for me to lie on?
Can I lie on that bed all stretched out, or confine myself to a fetal position waiting for a rebound?
Can I really love and be loved in return, or will love only to be a dream that is never real?
Pass the weed and allow me to escape, and rest for a while because reality is wiping me out

Everything Is Just Fine

Do we know or do we care?
I'm Black, I'm Brown, and somewhere in-between
People call me names in order to defame
The nation is in a shamble
Education nowhere to be found
Medicine man here and medicine man there
Medicine man, nowhere to be found
Job are hiding and Wall Street is a thriving
Inside the gated community, everything is just fine
Children starving and old folks dying
But politicians say, that everything is just fine
Money running short or not at all
Don't worry, my banker says everything is just fine
People are on the roof getting ready to jump but,
everything is just fine.

Face in the Mirror

The face in the mirror is never the same
It is always possible to grow uglier each day
The people were living nature's way
They were in harmony with the land
The ships came and touched the shores
The guns kept firing, and almost all were dead
The land was stolen fair and square
Now it's time to rape the land everywhere
Destroy the grassland, and allow the soil to blow away
Clear cut the mountain tops and the sides as well
The protection is gone, and the soil blows away
Gouge the land everywhere, and search for black gold
The oily stuff that brews pollution in the skies above
The sun and winds are the pipe dreams of the caring
Go to war again and again, and keep the blood flowing on the ground
Bring home the dead, and the broken bodies of the willing
There is never too high a price to pay for the greed that is abounding
Oh face in the mirror can change be so dreadful, or was it meant to be that way?

Fading Fast

War time, war time, and no peace to be found
Children dying and bullets flying
Reaching down and no reaching out
The weather is getting hotter
And the water is drying up
Crops dying in the field and no avail
No jobs and idle hands abound
Guns are blazing and young men dying
Drugs everywhere, and the only hope is fading fast

Fall

Summer has come and gone
And now it's time for the leaves to fall
The clouds are bringing some cover
The air seems to be a little cooler
Tempers are taking a retreat
Hand holding seems to be the theme
More smiles displayed along my walk
A peaceful mood has taken it's stance
Fall is the season among seasons
And my most favorite of all

Fallen Branches

Fallen branches drop their anchor on the ground
Their mighty branches were full of leaves not so long ago
Time has passed, and now they lay naked on the ground
The branches were once a resting place for birds on high
The branches were sunshades for those resting below
They provided the musical instruments for the wind as it passed through
They are now just broken logs and sticks on the ground
Are these magnificent branches destined for the fire pits?
Why can't they be restored as beautiful pieces of art?
Even as they are lying on the ground, I remember when they stood
so high

Fast-Moving Train

A nation appears to be falling like a cannon ball over the parapets of time
Ignorance is always falling down like a carpet preparing for the wake
The light seems to be spiraling out of sight, and dimness is our only delight
The divide is growing wider with no end in sight
Hate, deceit, and greed are now displayed on the marques up and down the street
Hands are covering the ears, and closed minds are encased in cement
People are running with the intent of finding a cliff high enough for the final assault
Others are running to locate the caves before they all fill up
The few that cared have long ago been shuttered out
The oceans are rising and the heat is growing hotter
The fresh waters are drying up, and thirst is on display
The minds are being thrown into the dungeons of mediocrity
Solutions are condemned, and are being classified as a disease
Mayhem is no longer hiding its evil face, and everything is in play
People starving and dying in the streets, and the homeless wander about
Faith is being crushed like a grape in the hands of a giant
This was once a different land, but now the landscape is changing
The fast-moving train of time is changing everything, and time has about to run out

Flexibility of the Mind

Flexibility of the mind can lead you to places you thought you
would never be
It doesn't have to be a traitor to your core beliefs, but just another station
Flexibility can adapt to a better understanding of where you should be
The world of thought should neither be just black or white, but often just shades of gray
An opening of the mind allows you to give the other people's thoughts a chance to filter through
It will become amazing at how many new friends
will want to be with you
Your journey in life needs all the support it can deliver, so allow yourself an open window for others to come through
An opening of the mind provides a pillow for others to rest on
Don't be afraid to allow others a change to love your open mind
I am personally a work in progress on the flexibility of the mind

Flowers in My Garden

Flowers in my garden
What a delight
The colors are beautiful
And the count is high
Never do I pick
Because it would be a shame
The picture would never be the same
Rows and rows all shades and hues
Standing like statues
So proud to express their beauty

Freedom

Does freedom come before I am done?
Is freedom just a word which should mean nothing to me?
Will freedom bring me riches, or just peace of mind?
Will freedom paint a new picture in me, or pass me by?
Will freedom give me tranquility and newness in my soul?
Is it possible to really be free when so many are placing ties on me?
How many rungs are in the ladder of freedom?
Is there really ever a top, or will the rungs always deceive me?
There is freshness in me which urges me to climb on
Each day is a new day; so I must encourage myself to go on
The birth of free will has always resided in me
I have always been free because freedom is within me

Freedom Speaks

Freedom is an allusion because it never really totally comes
There is always a new challenge waiting at the door of time
Good health today, but what about tomorrow?
It is always good times until the bad times drain the day
Where did the youth go because it was there not so long ago?
Making money, but how much is enough?
Migration further North as the weather takes hold of me
No cane for me today, but who took my cane for my tomorrows?
Please don't wheel me, but let me walk every mile during my time
Freedom tells me to never give up, but keep the allusion alive

There is not as much joy in this poem as there are in many of my poems, but it is reality.

Friend or Foe

Is death a friend or a foe?
Does it really know when to come or when to let go?
Is death just a word or a reality which seems to come all too soon?
Life isn't always an easy road to travel up or down
Is there really any mercy in knowing that end is near?
Why the suffering and not more mercy as you move toward our bedside?
Are you really the light and not the darkness which all too many fear?
Is there not any sunshine in your word to comfort us?
Are you my friend which I can trust to move me to a better place?
If you are my friend; then embrace me
Replace my fears with joy as the end is near

Garden of Caring and Love

Why is the garden of caring and love so hard to grow?
Past bitterness's do play a role, don't they?
Brushing off past hurts and restoring even a drop of love is something you must do
The must do is for you because anger only hurts you
The stain of hurt and anger often becomes the weeds in your garden.
Those weeds stop everything good from growing
Pain often just grows more pain, and you are the one that becomes painted with stain of hate
Remember that once the streams of love and caring begin to take hold; then it became impossible to stop
The small streams gather the force of others, and become a river, and that river will flood your heart into the world of change
Becoming a powerful river will set you free to open your heart once again
You will soar as you have never been able to soar before
You are a winner and always have been a winner
Lift that winning banner high; because you have again allowed yourself to grow
Soon, a beautiful garden of love and caring, is glowing for all the world to see
Your garden will soon allow others to follow your lead and grow their own gardens as well

Garden of Roses

There is much beauty in my garden of roses
Their deep colors are eye candy as never seen before
There is no need to take them from their garden home
Let them stay and welcome others in their beautiful way
The morning sun pulls back the curtain of darkness
It's time to view the garden again; as if it was never seen before
Roses each have a perfume of their own
They are flowers for the ages, and they have always been deep in my heart
Standing there viewing them brings back memories of a welcome past
Sharing the roses with others is the way it's meant to be
A garden of roses is nature's way of painting a picture for you and me

Get Hold of Your Self

Get hold of yourself and hold on tight
The troubles are here and more are to come
The climate is changing, and the price we are paying is mighty heavy
The cultural malaise is from coast to coast
The statues are falling to the ground
The threats are all over the world with no end in sight
The boys and girls in Washington are bending their elbows as fast as they can
Their minds are teetering on destruction, but the drinks keep coming
The dome building stands as a citadel to so little good
The old white building is decaying on the inside and out as insanity is the order of the day
The rainbow has been relegated to storybooks

Glow a/k/a happy

Stretch out the arms and offer a hug today
There are people waiting for your expression of caring
Smiles are always a welcome sight
Walk with love in your heart and people will feel it
Say something nice because it's the right thing to do
Yes, you are suffering and so are we all
There are always others suffering more just around the corner
Giving is a lifetime project and not just for today
Lift people up and never push them down
The sun is always shining when you are all aglow

Gone Again

I am back before I'm gone
But soon I will be gone again
I have no idea when I will be back
Gone is good, although I will miss my friends
Maybe I will make new friends
New places and sights to be seen
Travel has its price, and that might not be nice
It's worth the gamble because it may be alright
The is coming so I must say good-bye
I may even write in the by and by

Good Fortune

What good is money if you don't do something good with it?
Be the master of your money, and spend it wisely
Don't be afraid to share, but vet the receivers well
The good fortune of wealth should be a blessing for others, as well as yourself
Sit down and think for a while about your blessings if wealth
comes your way
No one comes by wealth alone, and not even in winning the lottery
The lottery win comes from the loss of others, which have foolishly thrown
their money your way
No one is an island unto themselves because everyone has always received help
along the way
Maybe you were blessed with good health and a powerful brain
Maybe you received a good education as a tool that brightened your pathway
along the way
Maybe your parents had the means to send you down the road
for more gain
Maybe the workers lifted you up, and made up something you could not
have done alone
Don't ever be so self-righteous, and proud that you stand alone, on a pedestal
that others have made
Sharing is not a bad idea because remember you didn't do it alone

Goose Bumps

Goose bumps are breaking out as the sounds are wrapped into my soul
A new being arises as each melodious sound flows through the air
The notes one after each other with their ups and downs
Finally reaching an even flow to calm the soul
It's the percussion, horns, and woodwinds in a beautiful blend
The woodwinds have their own special contribution to even out the sound
The saxophones, clarinets, flutes, oboe, piccolo, and let us not
leave out the bassoons
Life without music would leave us in desert always attempting to
find our souls

Music! Music! And more music! Always music

Gray

Is caring worth the while, or is it a burden to hide?
Loves only a word without any feeling?
Is smiling a sign of weakness, or something to share?
Are others worth the time, or are they only statues blocking your way?
Is understanding often lost in translation?
Alive, does it have a theme or reason for being?
So many questions to ponder, but do they have to be answered today?
Answers develop and may have meaning along the way
Yes, maybe today is not the day
The road can be long, and often the answers are in gray

Green

Green Is the Color of My Day
I woke up this morning and I was green from head to toe
The mirror said good morning soldier green
No black, brown, white, yellow, or red here, only green
Green is the only color a soldier knows
Green in the trenches and green in the halls
Green on the fields those battles know all too well
Went swimming in the bay, but the green was there to stay
Someone said you don't look green to me
I thought to myself with sadness in my eyes
If they were only soldiers then how green I would be

Happiness

Is happiness an illusion or real?
You are the only one which can foster happiness in your life
It all up to you to accept happiness or despair
Others cannot bring unhappiness into your life unless you allow this transition
People relationships are always a risk, but you are in charge of the risk
Tread lightly, but don't be afraid to tread
The pathway is rarely a straight line
There will always be curves in the road
It's alright to take a detour and move on
Some roads just have too many bumps
There are times when solace will be your best friend
Accept life a day at a time
If today is lived well, then tomorrow will be a better place in which to live

Happiness Is the Goal

Can I make you happy by telling you each day how much I love you?
Or, is words just beautiful poetry traveling in empty air?
Can your happiness depend only on you?
Then, can my niceties contribute to your tranquility?
Will my soft embrace provide you security?
Will a walk together in the moonlight furnish serenity to your soul?
Can I at least in some small way be a support to your pathway in life?
Can we travel down the pathway hand in hand and never letting go?
Can we never hide our love, but spread it each day on one another?
Can we cherish the goodness in our lives, and push the woes aside?
Can we look back at the good times, and know that there are more to come?
We will see the beautiful flower in us and each day watch it unfold?
Remembering each day that happiness is the goal.

Here

Where is the here because it is so difficult to recognize it as if it were a changing cloud
How did it come to be that I cannot seem to understand how it disguised itself so well?
The here slivered into the now like a thief in the night without revealing itself
Change is always changing, but the change is now moving so fast, much like a whirlwind, that is hard to grasp
Is humanity real or only an illusion as technology pushes it aside?
Is tomorrow today and the clock now has no relevance as time races by?
Am I real or just a piece in the museum of time?
Is the spinning wheel of change destroying all the reality that has always been in my mind?
How do the people massage themselves into the here as time passes them by as if they were not here?
As a person I attempt to be here, but technology says I am yesterday, and reality is not going to wait for me
Hanging on and adjust to the here, and attempting to find my place, as the swirl wind has consumed me

Holding on For Better Days

I used to be able to look out my window, and occasionally view a little normal reality
Now when I look out the window there is nothing there
It's like being in a time warp
The nation is rapidly becoming an empty vessel with an absence of meaning
There is no right or wrong because it is what it is
People moving about aimlessly, and there is no direction
It's a never-ending circle with no compass in sight
Everything in a free fall, and it's hard to hold on
Where are the people that use to care?
The people that use to nurture the future with a roadmap in hand
The spinning around continues, as in a tunnel with no end
Do I close the window and pull the shades?
Or is it all in my imagination, and better days are ahead?

Hollywood

I am going to Hollywood to make a movie
My golly my man, what's it going to be about?
It's about stuff and a little scary indeed
It's about truth which is something no one wants to know about
I have my director all lined up because he knows his way about
He knows his stuff and that's something to shout about
My material background and script are all worked out
My producers could be a problem, but I'll work it out
Will it make any money? Oh! There is no doubt
But truth is hard to sell; so will it be a soft sell?
Don't nay me, because it has been on my mind a long while
My contacts are waiting for my arrival; so I shouldn't delay
It's been on the table too long they say
You know Hollywood will surely love me
It's got to be that way

Hope

Hope is a word which springs forth a fountain of renewal
Hope is a joy and a treasure which elevates the spirit of one's soul
Hope searches for reality at every turn, and never looks back
Always hold on to hope, and encourage it to go on in search of more unimaginable goals
Hope always searches for higher ground, and the mountain is never high enough
The pull backs are always there to discourage your journey to a better place
March on and increase the pace because the climb has more hope waiting for you
Look around because there are more people about to join you
You are no longer alone because hope is a contagious thing

Hope for Better Days

Wild horses and freedom in the wind
Those days are behind us and a new day has begun
The hustle and bustle is all around us
Around and around we go with no end in sight
A little progress here and there, but the goal is never near
Freedom has been replaced by fear
Money everywhere, but never enough to spare
People are falling down, and they can't get on their feet
Remind them it's self-reliance that they need to meet
What do you mean they don't have enough to eat?
Doing with less is something they will have to meet
What do you mean some houses are too large, and some have none at all?
Sleeping on the streets is something they will have to meet
Times are tough and what's mine is mine
And sharing is something we don't wish to meet
Remember wild horses and freedom in the wind
That was yesterday and you may never meet them again
Things can change you know, and I am so hoping that it's so
Maybe better days are in the wind and we can all win

I Always Knew Them

I have known them for many years
But, I have never met them
Confusion or a conundrum
Or just a play on words
No, just reality, allow it to settle in
Served in the lines for so many years
Yes, have been here and there
So often where they were other where
My life and theirs was often in the same place
When we met we already knew each other

This is dedicated to the Armed Forces members whom I have known, but never met. If you have never served; then it may only be a conundrum, or just a play on words.

I Had a Beautiful Dream

I had a dream that peace, and tranquility stretched across the earth
People were kind, and compassion flowed around the globe
People were helping people, and always lifting them up
No one was ever being pushed down and never found
There was no hunger or homelessness that came into view
The oceans were never rising, but kept in bounds
The temperatures were pleasant and never gaining ground
The skies were clear, and the waters were drinkable everywhere
Diseases that we once knew were no longer there
Medical care was abundant, and everyone was getting well
Drugs, alcohol, and smoking were a thing of the past
The doors were never locked because no harm ever came our way
Serenity always had a home in our hearts that we held so dear

Nostalgia

When will the yesterdays be returning to me?
Have they gone to a place so far away?
The remembrance seem like only across the room
Those yesterdays were so very good to me
The memories are like a soft and gentle brush with time
The carefree time with friends and the beach was always nearby
The warm breeze from the ocean flooded my soul with a renewal each day
It was a magic city with all its majesty
Much like the storybooks from the times of old
Is my nostalgia removing me from the unrest that is always around me today?
Is this escape from reality what I need for a time or should I fade away into the prison of today

Tears

Tears come from many directions and often in mysterious way
There are tears of joy and tears of sadness
Sometimes tears appear without any reason at all
Some people laugh to hide the tears away
Tears are truly the lotion of the soul
Let the tears flow if the need is there
Weak or strong has no play here because it is your call
Live life your way and if tears fall then that is the way it is meant to be
Tears can bring relief even if the tears really never fall
Sometimes you may need the strength of others to pull you through
Hold on to others even if it is for a short while because even the strong need a rest
Rainbows are real and you are the pot of gold at the end

The Canoe and the River

The river is like no other means of travel
I really mean a smaller river where canoes can find a welcome trail
The river can be easy and lazy or a torrent stream
The up country can bring down strong waters from a heavy rain
Every bend brings new sights that have never before been seen
The trees grow, the flowers bloom, and the sun comes and goes
Small gentle white waters greet us today just around the bend
They are not too difficult to navigate, but still a challenge my friend
Watch out our for the larger rocks, and move around them
Did you see the beautiful birds watching us from the trees?
We are just one in one with nature as we make our way down stream
We are moving under an old abandon railroad trestle
It's just another sight to be seen
You can travel this river a thousand times, but it is never the same
The river to me is just an old friend
It needs to be visited from time to time
Memories of past travels are passing through my mind
It's difficult to leave the river, and maybe my travels should last a few more miles
My spirits are always heighten as the canoe moves along
My exit from the river will hopefully last only a short while

The Ground Is Not So Bad

Poor old, Humpty Dumpty, has had so many falls off that wall
It has happened so many times that the count is lost in time
The people say they remember, Humpty Dumpty, lying on the
ground in 1929
Humpty had been there many times before the fall of 1929
Every time the poor fellow gets up off the ground, then it is readiness time
for the next fall
Humpty, seems to spend more time on the ground than the wall above
The mint juleps are flowing down Washington's way
Humpty can always wait for another day
The ground is not so bad, because Humpty needs to rest
There are so many lobbyists to greed, and parties to attend

The Last Dance

I hear the roar of the ocean
The smell of the ocean is all around
The beach cannot be far away
Is it too early to return?
Will the floor of the sand be ready for the dance?
It's been so long, and do I know how it will all begin?
Will I have a partner this time?
Or just the wind
The air is crisp with cold of the Northwest
The beach is almost clear
But, this time will she be there?
Yes, her hair and dress are flowing in the wind
And her beauty is unsurpassed
Her moves are like the wind
She reaches out, and now we are hand in hand
The dance is about to begin
The twirls and the moving in and out
Her smile and laughter make it all worth while
Suddenly she moves away as the tide comes in
I cannot leave because this is my last dance

The Mountain Road

The mountain road is a beautiful ride
There is scenery everywhere with an ever changing view
The road moves from one side to another with no end in sight
Travel the road as many times as you like
It is impossible to determine if the next turn is to the left or right
In winter the road is a blanket of white
Spring brings a freshness of green everywhere in sight
There is coolness on the mountain road in summer as you go to greater heights
The road is a myriad of colors as fall comes into sight
A place of solitude overcomes one as you pull off the road
Reflections are easy to come by in the peacefulness of the mountain road

The No Mores!

Where did all the trees go, the ones that once covered the land
There used to be greenery everywhere, but now all there is bland
Buildings, roads, and concrete jungles everywhere
Trees have all been cut down to the bone, and difficult to find anymore
Where have all the trees gone you ask again?
They have been crushed, and swept away by the landslides, just yesterday
The fire has engulfed them, and burned them to the ground
The trees used to cover the landscape, but no more

The Waves and the Sand

The tides come in and the tides go out
The waves play a beautiful song on the shore
Sometimes there is loudness in the roar
Others times the waves have a more gentle song to play
The lull of the waves has a mesmerizing way to capture the soul
Stay the night for there no reason to abandon the sand
The cool breeze and ocean spray will provide more reasons to stay
The blanket on the sand with a beautiful lady in hand
Oh! The memories of that night will never leave my mind

What does it take to fill an Empty Heart?

Filling an empty heart can be a daunting task
Is it due to a love lost, or need for the gain of love?
No matter, because the pain remains the same
Does it require open arms, and a wiliness to take a chance?
The shell is often difficult to break and moves into an open space
Do you let your guard down or do you always keep your space?
The is often confused as to which moves it should make
Out stretched arms or a standing in place can be a strange place
Is filling an empty heart really worth the dangers that are lurking in place?
Some people never make the move, and others make too many moves
Love and filling an empty heart is possibly about all relationships
Friendships and love are really not that far apart
Filling an empty heart can require multitude of people and not just one
There is not an answer that can serve everyone
The person in the end that you must rely on is only yourself

About the Author

Thomas Hagan was raised in Miami, Florida. He began his military career in the United States Marine Corp. Later, he changed branches and served many years in the Medical Department of the United States Army before he retired at the rank of Colonel. Dr. Hagan was not very good at retirement and went on to continue his quest for knowledge and imparting it at the University of Alabama - Birmingham Medical School, where he served on the faculty for several years. He ended his career teaching high-school and middle school science courses. He currently resides in Tampa, Florida.

www.ingramcontent.com/pod-product-compliance
Lightning Source LLC
Chambersburg PA
CBHW072039110526
44592CB00012B/1478